# THE PARKING LOT

I0141354

*Adam Szymkowicz*

**BROADWAY PLAY PUBLISHING INC**
New York
www.broadwayplaypub.com
info@broadwayplaypub.com

THE PARKING LOT
© Copyright 2021 Adam Szymkowicz

Cover image: Drew Makepeace

First edition: June 2021
I S B N: 978-0-88145-904-3

Book design: Marie Donovan
Page make-up: Adobe InDesign
Typeface: Palatino

THE PARKING LOT was first produced by Mirrorbox Theatre in C S P S Hall, Cedar Rapids, Iowa, running from 18-26 September 2020. The cast and creative contributors were:

J...................................................................Marcia Hughes
TERRY............................................................. Scot Hughes

*Director*........................................................Cavan Hallman
*Stage Manager*................................................Chelsea White
*Sound Designer* ..................................................Bri Atwood
*Lighting Designer*......................................................Jim Vogt
*Crew*........................................................Kelly Shriver Kolln


THE PARKING LOT was also produced by Majestic Repertory Theater in Las Vegas, running from 24 September-11 October 2020. The cast and creative contributors were:

J...................................................................Natalie Senecal
TERRY.......................................................... Mike Vargovich

*Director*.............................................................Troy Heard
*Production design*...................................The Design Ninjas
*Parking lot provided by Fortis Auto Group*

# CHARACTERS & SETTING

TERRY, *male*
J, *female*

*A parking lot.*
*Time: The present*

*Note: The idea for this play is that during the pandemic, people can sit in the safety of their cars and watch these two actors, who in real life are quarantined together. I imagine we need mics on the actors and either the people in the cars can tune in to listen or we have speakers so everyone can hear well.*

*Cars can be positioned in one long line or to make a thrust stage.*

*Or people are outside in lawn chairs more than 6 feet apart.*

*On the ground, in chalk, two sides. Pro and Con. It's okay if the audience can't see it exactly because the actors will shout "Pro" or "Con" before making a mark.*

Special thanks in no particular order to John and Rhoda Szymkowicz, Seth Glewen, The Gersh Agency, Tricia O'Toole, Tish Dace, Kristen Palmer, Wallace Szymkowicz. Elizabeth Bochain. Joe Kraemer.

Kip and Michael at B P P I.

Marsha Norman, Avriel Hillman, Kent Nicholson, Cavan and Troy and the folks at Mirrorbox and Majestic. Chinaza Uche. Sasha Bratt. Jacques Lamarre. Brendan Powers and Rachel Burttram at Tiny Theatre.

Thanks to Caitlin Zoz for the line, "It's hard to dream right now." Thanks to Natalie Senecal for the Post-Its idea at the end.

At Juilliard, Tanya Barfield, David Lindsey-Abaire, Enid Graham, Charlie Oh, John J Caswell Jr., Brittany Fisher, Alex Riad, Dominic Finocchiaro, Emily Feldman, Jahna Ferron-Smith. Evan Yionoulis, Richard Feldman, Kathy Hood, Jerry Shafnisky, Kaitlin Springston, Victoria Lyons, Andrew Rodriguez, James Gregg, Lindsey Alexander, Carson Crow.

Gwydion Suilebhan, the New Play Exchange and all those who left reviews there of this play: Michael Hilton, David Hansen, Ruben Carbajal, Robert Alexander Wray, Samantha Marchant, Donna Hoke, Cheryl Bear, Katarzyna Kathy Müller, Emily McClain, Toby Malone

Special thanks to the actors who helped me by performing in development readings of this play.

For Susan Louise O'Connor, not because this play has anything to do with her but because she is a rockstar and an amazing human, and a stellar actor and because she helped make so many of my plays happen and it's a crime it took this long to dedicate a play to her.

# ONE

*(J and* TERRY *enter and speak to the audience.)*

TERRY: One.

J: The question on the table. Should we get a divorce?

TERRY: Right. Because. Con.
*(Makes a mark in the "Con" column)*

J: I can't keep living with you.

TERRY: Right. Me too. But. Pro.
*(Makes a mark in the "Pro" column)*

J: I can't live without you.

TERRY: Yeah. That too.

J: And so.

TERRY: And so.

J: *(To audience)* Hello.

TERRY: A parking lot.

J: A play in twenty scenes.

TERRY: Either of us can propose a scene and no scene proposed can be refused.

J: I guess.

TERRY: To me a parking lot is a kind of limbo. So much time wasted walking to and from cars. So much time looking for a space a little bit closer. And that's what my life is like right now. I feel like nothing is working at all right now. Maybe it never will. Who can say? But for sure I feel like my career, my life and everything in it are just a parking lot right now. Nothing here to look forward to. Just a wasteland. A nothingness.

J: Okay, right sure, but also, the opposite. Because a parking lot is possibility. A parking lot is hope. If you build it, they will drive here. They will want to come. They will bring themselves, maybe their families. They will need a place to gather together. A parking lot above all is necessary. You have to put the car somewhere.

TERRY: Okay, but—

J: Even if you take public transportation, right? All those busses need a place to go. You need a parking lot at the train station. A parking lot is limitless possibilities.

TERRY: Okay, but—

J: No. You are not grateful. You don't recognize the opportunities presented to you. A parking lot is an empty canvas. A parking lot can be anything. It can be everything.

TERRY: Um. It's just I was talking about how my life is awful right now.

J: Because you're not grateful. You are healthy.

TERRY: Okay.

J: You are strong. Good looking. Safe. Well fed. You are okay.

TERRY: Yeah. Well. It's just—

J: I know. We all know. Let's not do that. Okay?

TERRY: Okay.

J: Really.

TERRY: Okay.

J: I mean it.

TERRY: This is J.

J: Hi.

TERRY: I'm Terry.

J: Yeah.

TERRY: We've been together…what?

J: A while.

TERRY: A good while. But like how many years now?

J: Let's not get into that.

TERRY: They may want to know.

J: They don't need to know.

TERRY: It's about us. This is all about us. They want facts, I'm sure.

J: They can get by with one less fact.

TERRY: Well. Anyway. Welcome to our life. Should we maybe warn them?

J: No.

TERRY: It might be helpful.

J: No warnings. We experience it together. We let them know. We are here with you. We will get through it.

TERRY: Right but—

J: We get through it together. Say it.

TERRY: You and me or us and them?

J: Humanity as a whole. Say it.

TERRY: "We get through it together."

J: Because why?

TERRY: I don't know why. Because we have to?

J: Yes.

TERRY: Because what else can we do?

J: Yes.

TERRY: Because of kindness.

J: Right.

TERRY: Even when people are awful.

J: Especially when.

TERRY: And it will all be okay.

J: I mean there's okay and there's okay.

TERRY: Are you talking about us now?

J: Yeah.

TERRY: I mean I can be I think someone worthy of love.

J: That's not what I'm saying. You need to stop.

TERRY: Worthy of your love.

J: Don't make it about that.

TERRY: You're making me feel worse.

J: I'm just trying to tell them the truth. We have problems. We don't have to pretend everything is fine just because this is public.

TERRY: Now I'm stressed out again.

J: Okay but we have to do the show, so… Go do your deep breathing.

TERRY: Don't tell me what to do.

J: Okay, but.

TERRY: I'll go do my deep breathing.
*(He goes off to the side to do deep breathing, maybe some light meditation.)*

J: We got a great show for you. That's what Kermit the Frog always said. I'm a great admirer of Kermit the Frog. But I guess I need some highbrow quotation so you remember you're at the theater consuming art. Like Shakespeare maybe or okay— Walt Whitman

said, "Keep your face always towards the sunshine and shadows will fall behind you."
*(She thinks about this.)*
I like that one. It's good for actors too but I think it applies to all of us. Don't worry. This won't go too long. I know some of you will need to use the bathroom. So we'll keep it short. But substantive. I think. Sometimes I think about how some things are totally forgettable, right? But other things stay with you forever and some of it is about who you are when you read that book or see that movie or hear that song. And what it means to you in that moment. Anyway, I just hope to give you some of that nourishment right now. It might not work for everyone, but if it even works for one person, just hits them right in the right moment and shifts something important… so that's why we do this. Even on a day like today. So. Let's start. No flash photography. No frisky business. You know we can see you too.

## TWO

J & TERRY: Scene Two!

J: Don't forget we have a good parking lot memory. Pro!
*(She makes a mark in the "pro" column.)*

TERRY: You mean—

J: Not the first time we met but the second, maybe.

TERRY: Oh. Okay. Sure. Right.

J: You don't remember.

TERRY: I remember.

J: Years ago.

TERRY: How many years ago?

J: They don't need to know that. A parking lot not unlike this one.

*(Into past versions of themselves.)*

TERRY: Hey, hi!

J: I can't right now.

TERRY: No, it's me, Terry.

J: Okay.

TERRY: We met at Madeleine's and Catherine's? Remember?

J: Oh. Right. Yes.

TERRY: I'm not some rando.

J: Right. You're a rando I met.

TERRY: I went to college with Catherine.

J: Cool. Cool.

TERRY: We're old friends.

J: Okay.

TERRY: You, here uh…

J: Shopping, yeah.

TERRY: You live near here?

J: I do.

TERRY: Me too.

J: I'm not going to tell you where.

TERRY: Whoa. Relax. Just saying hi.

J: Hi.

TERRY: Hi.

J: Okay then, Bye.

TERRY: Wait. Um. You want to maybe get a drink?

J: With you?

TERRY: Am I not your type?

J: Just to be clear, you're asking me on a date?

TERRY: I'm trying to do one thing a day that scares me. This might cover tomorrow too.

J: Um. Mmm. Uh. Oh. Yeah. Okay. Catherine has my number.

TERRY: Really? Great!

J: Yeah, okay.

TERRY: And if it's like a pity date never mind.

J: No, it wouldn't be a…it's just that I just got out of a relationship.

TERRY: Oh. When?

J: Two years ago and I'm not sure. Like. I might not be ready yet.

TERRY: I mean you should definitely try to date. Two years! Two years!!

J: Okay, yeah, but…

TERRY: I would be dating like the day after a breakup. I try to sleep my way out of the funk, you know.

J: Yeah. Okay.

TERRY: Too much information?

J: I mean that's not great, no.

TERRY: I didn't mean it like—

J: Call Catherine. We'll go get a drink, next week maybe.

TERRY: It's a date!

J: Yeah. That's what I just said.

## THREE

TERRY: It was a date. And then another and another and you wake up one day and years have passed.

J: Yeah.

TERRY: Our lives have passed. Our looks have gone.

J: No.

TERRY: Maybe no one would want us anymore.

J: No.

TERRY: We are old.

J: Not really.

TERRY: But also, am I my best self with you?

J: Best and worst.

TERRY: Oh.

J: I bring out all the things.

TERRY: And me?

J: You have no effect on me whatsoever.

TERRY: That's not— because, when your mother died.

J: I don't want to do that.

TERRY: It's important.

J: But.

TERRY: You have to and you have to do it well. Cause if you're not going to do it well…why do it at all. That's what you always say. See— You do bring out the best in me!

J: Fine. It was sudden. Unexpected. She wasn't young, but she was active. She played Tennis! But the cancer came fast and hard and it was over before anything could be done.

TERRY: In the hospital parking lot. I held you while you cried. It went on a long time. Eventually the tears subside. And I think, maybe we'll get in the car soon. Maybe we'll go home.

J: But when we're home it becomes real.

TERRY: Yeah.

*(Transition to the flashback)*

J: I don't think I'll ever recover.

TERRY: You will.

J: We talked every day. What am I gonna do when five o' clock comes? Every day will be hard. And Christmas? How can I have Christmas? Or Mother's Day. Children shouldn't outlive their mothers.

TERRY: It's going to be okay.

J: No.

TERRY: I'm here.

J: I know. I'm glad you're here.

TERRY: I know it hurts.

J: It does.

TERRY: But the pain will get better.

J: Will it?

TERRY: The weight will become lighter and more infrequent. We will get through this.

J: Okay.

TERRY: Every day. Until one day we don't notice we're just trying to get through the day and it's just a day again.

J: Yeah?

TERRY: And we'll be okay. It'll all be okay.

J: Okay.

TERRY: Say it.

J: It will all be okay.

TERRY: Yeah. Do you believe it?

J: A little.

TERRY: Good enough. Tomorrow, maybe a little more.

J: Okay. I love you.

TERRY: I love you.

*(Back to present)*

J: Whoo.

TERRY: That's a pro.

## FOUR

J: Four.

*(While* TERRY *talks,* J *sets up cones, maybe hoops, ramps.)*

TERRY: Some things, in life, just aren't possible and you have to reassess what can and can't happen. And think about what you want to leave behind. And what you're capable of leaving behind. Kindnesses— All of us can make moments of that— habits of that even. Although admittedly, it's much harder for some of us than others. Help? Help is helpful. Art. Art of course is a thing to make and leave behind. I'm trying to write a song right now. You want to hear it? Maybe in a minute. Some of us have skills we can use in service of others or we can teach to others. Money. You can give people money if you have money. I think, most importantly, just changing your mindset to try to help other people shifts the depression away from me. So then what are you doing? What do you want to do? What can you do? You want to hear my song?

*(Sings)*

I.

*(Starts again.)*

I.

*(Stops singing)*

I'm not ready yet.

J: Are you done?

TERRY: What's this?

J: Obstacle course.

TERRY: Obstacle course?

J: That's what I said. Put on the helmet.

TERRY: Helmet?

J: Stop repeating me. Put the kazoo in your mouth. I'll time you. You start there and end there. You balance on the and go up over that. You can do a jump for extra points. What else. Through there. You got that, right?* *(Note: Feel free to change words to explain actual course you build)*

TERRY: What am I doing?

J: Did you hear any of what I just said?

TERRY: Yeah but like you want me to run?

J: *(Pointing to the scooter)* The scooter.

TERRY: Oh. Okay.

J: I'll time you. Ready.

TERRY: Hold on.

J: You ready?

TERRY: Give me a minute.

J: …You ready?

TERRY: Okay.

J: Go!

(TERRY *does the obstacle course on the scooter. And then is done.*)

TERRY: Done! What was my time?

J: *(Tells* TERRY's *time.)*

TERRY: Go ahead and beat that!

J: Oh, I'm not doing it.

TERRY: What?

J: The obstacle course is just for you.

TERRY: What? I call foul. Foul! That's a con! You con artist.
*(He makes a line in the con section.)*
Look what you did? You took all the fun out of competitive scooter courses.

J: I could do it. I just don't want to. I don't feel like I have to prove something.

TERRY: And I do?


## FIVE

J: And Five!

TERRY: Five.

J: After the knockdown drag out fight to end all fights.

TERRY: We could show it to you, but honestly it's kind of boring. It's all—

J: "You don't listen to me."

TERRY: "You're not hearing me."

J: "I never said that."

TERRY: "Je t'accuse! Je t'accuse." That means I accuse you. In French. I took French.

J: Anyway… After the fight.

TERRY: Hours later. J goes for a walk.

J: Terry plays a video game.

TERRY: J returns.

J: Terry has paused already to get a snack.

TERRY: Their eyes meet.

J: Who will say something first?

TERRY: Not me.

J: Not me.

TERRY: They look at each other.

J & TERRY: Hey.

TERRY: So. For dinner I was thinking hamburgers. Or we could go out.

J: You want to sit across from me and have a meal someone else made?

TERRY: Maybe. I dunno. What do you think?

J: An hour ago I wanted to burn our apartment down. Now you're talking about hamburgers.

TERRY: Or cheeseburgers.

J: Yeah. That sounds nice but let's go out. But this doesn't mean the fight is over.

TERRY: We will have it again.

J: And again.

TERRY: Many of them in parking lots.

J: Restaurant parking lots. Grocery store parking lots. The Lowes parking lot. The Cheesecake Factory parking lot. *(Note: Replace with local lots if these don't apply)*

TERRY: It's not always the same argument. Sometimes it's about something else. But also it's about one thing.

J: "I am aggrieved!"

TERRY: "I am aggrieved."

J: You are aggrieving me! Stop being this way.

TERRY: You stop first.

J: And so you see.

TERRY: Con.


## SIX

J: Six. But also among our friends—

TERRY: What?

J: We're celebrities.

TERRY: Okay. In our field, too.

J: You mean theater?

TERRY: Yeah theater. That old dinosaur.

J: Like people talked about— Would they— Wouldn't they. Before we were together. Like as if we were in a gossip magazine. And then when we got together, they imagined us.

TERRY: Did they?

J: Like what was our home life? What fancy party are they at now? What T V show are they bingeing? I wish their parents were my parents.

TERRY: No.

J: I wish their lives were my lives.

TERRY: Really?

J: And I get it.

TERRY: You do?

J: We're totally charismatic.

TERRY: Right.

J: And attractive.

TERRY: Moderately.

J: And probably some of them were secretly in love with us.

TERRY: Wait, what?

J: Don't you think?

TERRY: No, who?

J: Kari.

TERRY: No.

J: Bob.

TERRY: Maybe. Lindsey?

J: Yeah.

TERRY: I mean you have a following.

J: So people care. About what happens with us. Maybe because they want to swoop in.

TERRY: You think?

J: Or because they love our love. It's a public relationship. In some ways. We had that podcast.

TERRY: Yeah. And you're very sexual.

J: What?

TERRY: You make people think about sex.

J: No. Really? No.

TERRY: Yeah. So I assume most of our friends have imagined us having sex.

J: What?

TERRY: Yeah.

J: No.

TERRY: Yeah.

J: Oh. That's—I'm not sure I like that.

TERRY: Anyways.

J: So I'm just saying. There's other people.

TERRY: Is that a pro or a con?

J: It's just a complication.

TERRY: Right. Like. Okay. Okay. Hmmm. I'm not adding that to either column.

J: Do you remember when we got married?

TERRY: Of course.

J: Everyone looking at us. Like really looking at us. I never felt so looked at.

TERRY: Never? Not even right now?

J: All of them, wanting to be me or you.

TERRY: Really? No. Really?

J: Yeah.

TERRY: No, but really? You really think that?

J: Sometimes. You were all, "I do".

TERRY: I do.

J: I do.

TERRY: I do.

J: Why did we get married?

TERRY: Uh. What? For like stability. And for home. And for trust.

J: Okay but.

TERRY: For gifts.

J: When we got into this, you said I could still leave at any time.

TERRY: I said that. To get you to agree to it. Because you didn't know. If it was a good idea. For you.

J: That's not true. You did it so you could get out too. If you had to.

TERRY: That's not fair.

J: It isn't.

TERRY: But fine. People divorce.

J: I know.

TERRY: If that's what you want… But J, really think about it J, because…

J: Can we stop the play for a second?
*(To the audience)*
I just want to say to you. You are worthy of love. Maybe you already know this. Or suspect it. Or maybe you don't really believe me. But I want to be sure you hear me. You are worthy of love.

Also you don't have to be afraid, which doesn't mean the world isn't sometimes scary but that within this crazy world, you deserve to be somewhere safe.

Also once in a while you deserve a treat. You deserve a parade when you do something amazing. You may not get one, but you deserve it.

Me, I only see the horrible things I've done or said or thought. Mostly I think I don't deserve any success or love but also at the same time I think I'm the most amazing person that has ever existed. So sometimes it's hard to be me.

## SEVEN

J: Seven

J & TERRY: Reasons for divorce

J: That noise you make when you clear your throat.

TERRY: Your sneezes.

J: Your socks.

TERRY: Your unctions. And lotions.

J: Your bad opinions.

TERRY: Your bad ideas.

J: Your obsession with goblins.

TERRY: Gnomes.

J: Whatever.

TERRY: It's not the same.

J: Okay. But.

TERRY: That time that you lied. Right to my face. I said, "Where were you last night?"

J: Which time?

TERRY: "Which time?" Did you just say "which time?"

J: I mean "what time?"

TERRY: How many times are we talking about? Ballpark.

J: Let's move on.

TERRY: Yeah. Knowing that you don't love me enough. You will never love me enough. But also maybe no one ever will but definitely you won't.

J: Ouch.

TERRY: Yeah. Your depression.

J: Your anger.

TERRY: Your toilet paper rule.

J: Your inability to be loved.

TERRY: Your pillows.

J: Your wardrobe.

TERRY: Your issues with authority.

J: When you don't shave.

19

When you prevent me from being me.
When you consume me.
When you don't listen.
When you don't hear.
When you. When you. When you…when—

TERRY: Is it over?

J: Con!
(*She makes a mark.*)

## EIGHT

TERRY: Eight. So. My song. Wanna hear it? I think now maybe, yes. I think…I. I. I. I. I'm gonna try again later.

## NINE

J: Nine! Con! BETRAYAL!!!
(*Makes a mark in the "Con" column.*)

TERRY: In the parking lot outside our friend's building.

J: Betrayal!

TERRY: Nothing happened.

J: What does that mean? Did something happen?

TERRY: I'm saying nothing happened.

J: Yes but why are you saying that?

TERRY: In case you thought that.

J: What are we talking about?

TERRY: I thought you thought. Never mind.

J: What do you not want me to know? Something happened?

TERRY: Nothing happened.

J: Yeah but what happened? You were in the kitchen with Rosie.

TERRY: She might have. Kissed me.

J: Her? You like that kind of girl?

TERRY: No.

J: You think she's pretty?

TERRY: No. I just was talking too close maybe or she misunderstood or she was drunk.

J: Okay. You don't wish I looked like that?

TERRY: No. God no.

J: Okay, then. Okay. Then, I don't care.

TERRY: You don't care? You should care!

J: No, I care. I care. I kind of care.

TERRY: That's fine with you? You don't care who I kiss?

J: You said she kissed you.

TERRY: Right.

J: Did you kiss her or did she kiss you?

TERRY: She kissed me.

J: You sure?

TERRY: Yeah.

J: Because…

TERRY: Because what?

J: It's been a while for you and me.

TERRY: For.

J: Yeah for intimacy?

TERRY: It wasn't a real kiss.

J: Show me.

TERRY: Now?

J: Yeah.

TERRY: How?

J: Show me.

(TERRY *kisses J.*)

TERRY: See. Nothing.

J: Do it again.

(TERRY *kisses J.*)

TERRY: Yeah but less tongue.

J: There was tongue?

TERRY: Maybe.

J: BETRAYAL!

TERRY: No.

J: BETRAYAL!!

(TERRY *stops* J *with a kiss. They kiss. They kiss. The argument is over, maybe.*)

J: Okay. As long as it wasn't like that. Also, we are never going over that apartment again.

## TEN

J: Ten. Checklist version twelve
Do they
make me laugh
make me dinner
excite me sexually
dance for me
read to me
sing to me?

Are they
soft
hard

kind
rational
well dressed
well informed
fun to be around
adventurous
good with pets
good with children
good with houseplants
good at rock climbing
smarter than me
dumber than me
older than me
younger than me
wiser than me
taller than me?

Would you miss them?

Do you love them?
Do they smell good?
Do they say excuse me?
Do they seem happy to see you?
Do they know all your passwords?

Is this list too long?

Am I asking too much?

Do they know you?

Do you know them?

Do they make you think?

Do they make you wonder?

Do they make you happy?

Do they make you happy?

Do they make you happy?

## ELEVEN

TERRY: Eleven. On the way back to our car from a hike up to a waterfall. It was a long hike but it was worth it right?

J: Yeah.

TERRY: But now we're back in the parking lot and you say—

J: Thanks for suggesting we come here.

TERRY: Yeah.

J: It's very beautiful.

TERRY: Right. Good. And later we'll have dinner.

J: Yeah. We've been together a while now, huh?

TERRY: Yes.

J: I'm getting an energy from you.

TERRY: Oh!

J: And this isn't my first rodeo.

TERRY: What number rodeo is it?

J: Let me make something clear, just in case you have designs. I'm not a homemaker.

TERRY: Like a carpenter?

J: I'm not going to cook and bake and take care of children.

TERRY: Okay.

J: You understand?

TERRY: You don't want children?

J: Well I don't know. I'm just saying I'm independent and I wouldn't quit my job or something.

TERRY: Okay.

J: And I don't believe in marriage as an institution. It's just a thing men made up to own women. And sure maybe it's other things now. I won't argue the point but it's still sexist and wrong. And so people can say, "my wife" or "my husband." Like see this person here? I own this person. This person belongs to me. But people shouldn't belong to other people.

TERRY: Okay.

J: So before you get any ideas, think again.

TERRY: Okay.

J: Because I am a free person and I will not be tied down to some backwards institution and make my friends buy matching outfits and buy me presents.

TERRY: Presents!

J: And I mean who can afford it. So yes, we've been together for a long time and people are wondering. And yes if I want to have children I should start the process tomorrow. But do I? Wouldn't I just mess them up?

TERRY: I don't think you would do that.

J: So I see you, all dressed up and I see you with a lump in your pocket and so I'm saying plainly do not propose to me today, tomorrow, at all, ever.

TERRY: I hear you. I do. Also. I'm gonna do it anyway. Just see what happens. You are the most important person in my life and I can't live without you and I want to know.
(*Gets down on one knee*)
Will you marry me.

(*J stares at* TERRY.)

TERRY: Is that a—

J: YES!

## TWELVE

TERRY: Twelve! I think I can sing my song now.
Actually could you just look away for a second?
I'm trying to imagine you're all naked or puppies
or something but it's not working. Just. Look at
something else. Great. Great. Hhhhhhhhh. No. I can't
do it. I'll try again later. Later.

## THIRTEEN

J: Thirteen.

TERRY: The first time I broke up with you.

J: We don't need to show them that. Also, what are you
talking about? You never broke up with me.

TERRY: I mean a couple times I have, yeah.

J: When? What? Okay. Okay. I see how you could think
that. I mean, yeah, I made you think maybe that you
were the one breaking it off.

TERRY: I broke up with you.

J: Well, did you though?

TERRY: I'm about to do it again.

J: Fine. You tell it your way. I'll sit here quietly.

TERRY: Promise?

J: I'm not saying anything.

TERRY: The first time I broke up with you, you were
looking out the window. Go look out the window.

(J *pretends to look out the window.*)

J: I'm looking at my car. Parked. Why do we own
things? Then I have to worry about something
happening to my car or my—we shouldn't own things.

TERRY: You were looking out the window. You were wearing that shirt that I hate and I felt trapped but also alone. You started to do the dishes. I was going to come up behind you, maybe kiss your neck but instead I said— I think we should break up.

J: Oh right. Yeah. I goaded you into that.

TERRY: What?

J: You only said that because I wanted you to. And then you felt guilty and I had the upper hand. And I've had the upper hand ever since.

TERRY: Fourteen.

J: What?

TERRY: Scene Fourteen!


## FOURTEEN

(J *and* TERRY *carry on a couch. He lies on the couch, maybe puts on a blanket, has a remote in hand. She enters with shopping bags.*)

TERRY: Where were you? I need you.

J: Grocery store.

TERRY: Oh, I hate that parking lot. People always come out of nowhere and surprise you and you're like where did you come from? I'm always just almost getting into an accident there.

J: Yeah.

TERRY: How'd you do?

J: Good. Fine. They were out of some stuff.

TERRY: I need your help.

J: Yeah, let me just put the groceries away.

TERRY: Can it wait?

J: Well.

TERRY: You get ice cream?

J: No.

TERRY: It can wait then.

J: I guess technically. It's just that I want to put them away.

TERRY: I get that. I do. It's just that I need you for something.

(*J gives up, sits next to* TERRY *on the couch.*)

J: Okay. What's up.

TERRY: So this may sound…crazy.

J: Yeah, that's what I assumed.

TERRY: My biggest fear is that you will die and I won't be able to go on with you gone.

J: That's your biggest fear?

TERRY: Yes.

J: I mean that's kind of nice.

TERRY: I don't want to live in this fear. Can you…what if you pretended to be dead and I mourn you and eulogize you?

J: And this will help you?

TERRY: I think so. And also, I'll say all the nice things about you now so you hear them when you're alive. So if you could just lie down there.

J: Here?

TERRY: Yeah. And play dead. Good. You're good at that. Okay. Thanks everybody for coming here to celebrate J today. J is…was spectacular. But you already know that. You all have your own stories probably about amazing things she did to help you move or get over a breakup or sat with you and held

your hand that one time in the hospital. But I want
to tell you about something you might not know
about. I want to tell you about the notes. Because she
leaves notes everywhere. To tell me things of course,
like "Went for a run." Or "Pick up dry cleaning." But
also, among the forks, you might find, "Remember
the universe is infinite." You might find quotes from
Shakespeare or from books or movies. You might find
a thought about something out of context. You might
find a love note for you among the frozen peas. You
might see a picture and some words in French on the
back. A quote from Plato. A memory about J's mom.
A tiny watercolor in a cardboard frame. A collage on a
three by five card. A poem.

And you know even now, I bet I'll still find one in a
shoe I haven't worn in a while or at the bottom of my
shirt drawer, under the sink, behind all the cleaning
supplies, behind the couch maybe. And each note will
be a new treasure, a piece of J I can still have. But there
will be no new notes. And because of that, I may never
recover.

J: Thanks. That was surprisingly moving.

TERRY: Yeah.

J: Did that help?

TERRY: Yeah.

J: Good. Also, you know you're dying first, right?

TERRY: What?

J: I'm definitely going to outlive you. So I'm the one
who's going to have to come to terms with your death.

TERRY: No. Oh. You're probably right. You want to
eulogize me?

J: No. I'm okay. I'll just move on to someone else after a
while. I do okay, you know, on the open market.

TERRY: Wow.

J: That's what they say. When they see me coming. They say "Wow."

TERRY: Okay Con.
(*Marking the ground*)

J: What? That was a pro-scene.

TERRY: It was and then you made it con.

J: Erase that.

TERRY: I will not. It properly expresses my feelings.

J: Okay. I'm putting two pros then.

TERRY: I'm putting three cons.

J: Let's just move on.

TERRY: Fine.

J: Fine. I don't want to give you a pro anyway.

TERRY: Fine.


**FIFTEEN**

J: Fifteen

TERRY: Reasons to stay together.

J: Your cooking.

TERRY: Your smells.

J: Your wit. That smile.

TERRY: Those eyes.

J: Sexual compatibility.

TERRY: You know me by now. I don't want to have to explain things to someone else.

J: Right. You love me

TERRY: You love me. Maybe. Even though

J: Even though

TERRY: All the terrible things about me.

J: Everything awful.

TERRY: And.

J: And.

TERRY: Also.

J: Also.

TERRY: I feel like there was something else. Right on the tip of my tongue. Uh. Hold on.

J: I have to step out of this play again for a minute. It's hard for me to dream right now. Nothing seems possible.

I want to be special like everyone else but unlike everyone else I know I'm not. I mean maybe I could have been at one point. I act of course and I think I'm good, and I do work at that but I wonder about other things I didn't do. Like studying to be a great artist or dancer. Or a doctor. If I had put in the effort. Woke up early and practiced like olympians do. But I never would have been that probably. Not really. So I'm just normal. Like you. And you. And you. And you.

But what I want is to daydream. I want time to read and look at the sky and read poems and I want to not be afraid. Can we just for one day put all the anxiety away and pretend we don't have to worry about money or living up to our potential or how to be human and just be. I want to just be and not feel guilty about it. Can I?

Okay.

Okay.

## SIXTEEN

TERRY: At your sister's wedding.

J: Can we not?

TERRY: At your sister's wedding. You were grumpy. I was tired. We couldn't sleep in the hotel bed the night before. There was a party next door.

J: It was my sister.

TERRY: And your mother wasn't there to see the day.

J: Yeah.

TERRY: And your sister was marrying an idiot.

J: Right.

TERRY: But you didn't tell me that yet. I just knew you were snapping at everything I said.

J: And I looked terrible and I felt—

TERRY: I almost said, to hell with this. I was looking at bus tickets. I was ready to walk away, go home and pack up. But then I saw your face. And you were crying. The reception had started and we were three songs in. I went to the D J and I asked him to play our song. And it came on and I stood next to you and I held out my hand and we danced.

(J *and* TERRY *dance.*)

J: And we fit together better than we ever had before. And I forgot about my sister's dumb decisions and Karen at work and I didn't think of how much I missed my mom or Dad making eyes at the caterer. We just danced. And danced. And we kept dancing.

TERRY: Yeah.

J: And held each other tight. And didn't let go.

TERRY: Yeah.

J: And went home together.

TERRY: And we were happy. Weren't we? Pro.

## SEVENTEEN

TERRY: Seventeen. That time we were separated.

*(Transition to their past selves)*

J: Hey.

TERRY: Hey.

J: Thanks for/

TERRY: Yeah.

J: meeting up.

TERRY: Yup.

J: Buy you a drink?

TERRY: Oh I'm not/

J: What?

TERRY: drinking now.

J: Oh.

TERRY: But you can get one.

J: No.

TERRY: I don't mind.

J: If I'd known, I would have/

TERRY: Yeah.

J: suggested another place.

TERRY: *(Beat)* So. How's things?

J: Like life without you?

TERRY: I guess. Or like work or whatever.

J: It's hard. Honestly, it's been hard.

TERRY: What do you miss most about me?

J: Why are you saying that? Are you trying to get back together?

TERRY: I don't know. Are you? Why did you ask me to come?

J: I thought. Maybe there were things to discuss. I thought. Is it over? Is this a break or a break?

TERRY: Well you did the breaking, so…

J: Yeah. But now—

TERRY: You want me back.

J: Maybe.

TERRY: I have conditions.

J: Excuse me, you have what?

TERRY: I can't handle your jealousies anymore. That has to change. If something good happens, I want to be happy for me instead of comforting you because you feel bad for you. Because sometimes it can be about me.

J: It's always about you.

TERRY: What?

J: When isn't it about you?

TERRY: Sometimes.

J: I reject that. I don't need to make you feel good all the time.

TERRY: That's not what I'm saying.

J: I'm not your caretaker. So either take me as I am or walk away.

TERRY: You mean just

J: Walk away.

TERRY: Yeah but you don't mean…

J: Walk away.

(J and TERRY transition out of the past.)

Terry: Con.

J: Yeah. That was a con.


## EIGHTEEN

J: Eighteen.

Terry: I've lost my way.

J: I know.

Terry: What if I'm useless?

J: You're not useless.

Terry: What if I'm just wasting oxygen. Maybe the world would be better without me in it. I've started thinking. What if—

J: Stop. If we have to go to a hospital right now, we'll go to a hospital. But you're not k—

Terry: Maybe it would be better.

J: No one comes out of that better. Everyone that knew you would be messed up. If you won't think of yourself, think of me. You know how hard that will be for me?

Terry: Yeah. Sorry. Really? Okay.

J: You are alive.

Terry: Okay.

J: Enjoy living.

Terry: Maybe.

J: Each breath is a gift. Take up space. And also? We need you here.

Terry: For what?

J: You make food.

Terry: Right.

J: You tell jokes.

TERRY: Okay.

J: You have knowledge to pass on.

TERRY: Okay. Like what?

J: You tell me. You have to do some of your own lifting.

TERRY: Okay. I know. Okay.

J: And also, keep talking to me. I'm here. We can
get help. You can always call me. Always. If I'm not
physically there. Always.

TERRY: Promise?

J: Yeah.

TERRY: But you're not good at answering your phone.


## NINETEEN

J: Nineteen. But I've been there for you too.

TERRY: Sometimes.

J: When you were in the hospital. Lie down. You're in
the hospital.

(TERRY *lies down on the couch. Or maybe stays sitting up
over the following.*)

TERRY: That was awful.

J: We haven't seen each other in what?

TERRY: Months.

J: And I get a call you're in the hospital.

TERRY: Who called you?

J: I think it was Catherine. And she told me. Broken leg.
Broken arm. And your face.

TERRY: I was really messed up. The car just came out of
nowhere. My bike was demolished. I was lucky to—

J: You were lucky. Hi.

TERRY: *(Lying down now)* Hi.

J: How you doing?

TERRY: Not great. I can't reach the—my drink.

J: You could call a nurse.

TERRY: I don't want to bother them. You hold the drink up to my lips.

J: You drink deeply.

TERRY: It's good to see you. I didn't think you'd come.

J: I almost didn't. And I sit and we talk for hours about us and other people and life and feelings. And good habits and bad habits and you make me laugh.

TERRY: I'm hilarious.

J: I know. I had forgotten that somehow. And then visiting hours are over and I kiss you on the forehead goodbye.

TERRY: I didn't know if that was good or bad. But it was nice. And you come back the next day.

J: I do. And then I move back in when you get out of the hospital.

TERRY: You stay. And you didn't leave again.

J: I take care of you. I get you back on your feet. And if you think that doesn't mean something.

TERRY: I didn't say that.

J: But also I'm so tired. Of all the heavy lifting. I just don't know if I can keep doing it. So that's. Yeah.

*(Beat. Sigh)*

## TWENTY

J: Twenty. Reasons To Fall In Love.

TERRY:  Sometimes you fall in love with someone maybe just because they're there.

J: That doesn't happen.

TERRY: That's what happened when you fell in love with me.

J: I fell in love with you because I love you.

TERRY: Okay.

J: Because of who you are.

TERRY: Yeah I know.

J: Because of your kindness. Because of your beautiful soul.

TERRY: All right.

J: I fell in love with the person you try to be but also who you already are and just don't know it.

TERRY: Really?

J: Really.

TERRY: Do you still feel that way?

J: Yeah, I do.

TERRY: So. Do you want to have a scooter race?

J: No.

TERRY: Because you know I'd win.

J: Because it doesn't matter. Sometimes it's not about moving around. It's about staying in one place. Park your car. Rest for a bit.

TERRY: Okay. Are we done? Should we look at the scoreboard?

J: We were gonna do that scene where I throw the drink in your face.

TERRY: Oh right. Do we have to?

J: I was looking forward to it.

TERRY: Let's just forget about that one.

J: Also the scene where you know, I walk in on you, you know.

TERRY: Let's definitely not do that.

J: And that time at the aquarium. The bowling alley. Your mother's second wedding.

TERRY: I mean there are a lot of moments.

J: Yeah.

TERRY: That define our relationship. But we can't judge all the birthdays and Christmases and Thursdays and all the high points and the low points. Eventually we add it up and we say yeah, that's what it is and that's what it isn't. So what is it? Do we just get in our cars and drive away from each other or is there something here to salvage?

J: Yeah. I mean our relationship has some things going for it right?

TERRY: Right.

J: It's not toxic. We have humor. We have kindness. And neither of us can be everything for the other one. You know that, right?

TERRY: Yeah.

J: Do you?

TERRY: Yeah.

J: So we can be sick to death of each other and tired of your socks on the floor. But people don't really change, do they?

TERRY: I can.

J: But do we love each other?

TERRY: Yes.

J: Do we like each other?

TERRY: Mostly.

J: You know what? When it comes down to it I know my life is better with you in it.

TERRY: Yeah. Okay. I feel that way too.

J: So then, that's the big one right?

TERRY: It's little but it's big. Okay. Pro.
*(Goes to make a mark.)*

J: No. Stop. That's done. Clean slate.

TERRY: Clean slate. Like really a clean slate?

J: Yeah. Let's just—

*(J and* TERRY *get buckets or powerful squirt guns. A hose. They methodically wash all the marks away. Until it is wet and clean and gone.)*

J: Clean slate.

TERRY: Clean slate. So that's done. So we're…

J: Still together.

TERRY: And in love.

J: Afraid so.

TERRY: Good. I wish we hadn't taken two cars.

J: *(To audience)* Thanks for coming.

TERRY: Yeah. Thanks for coming.

J: To this parking lot.

TERRY: I don't know if you're in a bad place, but hang in there, okay.

J: Yeah. Hang in there.

TERRY: The world needs you. It may not feel that way.
But it does.

J: And humanity isn't over yet. Even if it feels that way
sometimes. There's more to come.

TERRY: And you are welcome to contribute.

J: Invited, even.

TERRY: Go now. That's it. Right?

J: Yeah, that's it. Unless. Your song.

TERRY: Oh. I guess I could. It's just—I don't know if—

J: Look at me. You have value.

TERRY: Yeah.

J: It's worth it. Being vulnerable. Taking a risk.

TERRY: I know.

J: Take a leap. I'm right here.

TERRY: Right. This is my parking lot song. Wait one—
I'm gonna change a line based on the clean… Hold on.
I think, yeah.
(*Rearranges in his mind*)
Yeah. I. I. I.

(TERRY *sings. As he sings,* J *walks around sticking post it
notes on people's windshields, like the kind she leaves around
at home. They say inspirational things like "You matter",
and "You deserve love", and "The world needs you", and
"Hang in there", "Shine on", and quotes from literature. A
couple might have fortune cookie fortunes pasted on. Etc*)

TERRY: I was all I could see. But I wasn't a lot.
I don't know if I can, but I'll take a shot.
It's not all that I want, but it is what I got.
I found a clean slate for me in a parking lot.

The Parking Lot Frees You
The Parking Lot Sees You

The Parking Lot Loves You
The Parking Lot Is True

The Parking Lot's For Me
The Parking Lot's For You

You are all I could want. But I wasn't a lot.
I didn't know if I could, but I took a shot.
It was all that I want, and it is what I got.
I found a clean slate for us in a parking lot.

The Parking Lot Frees You
The Parking Lot Sees You
The Parking Lot Loves You
The Parking Lot Is True

The Parking Lot's For Me
The Parking Lot's For You

*(Spoken)* Everybody!

The Parking Lot Frees You
The Parking Lot Sees You
The Parking Lot Loves You
The Parking Lot Is True

The Parking Lot's For Me
The Parking Lot's For You

*(Spoken)* Thank you. I. I. Thanks.

J: Thanks. Bye.

TERRY: Bye.

END OF PLAY